Images of Modern America

BONNEVILLE'S WOMEN OF LAND SPEED RACING

Here starts the fun. Under the rainbow, on the frosted iridescence of hard-crusted salt—not snow—everyone begins the grasp for glory. Tires and shoes extract the same crispy, crunchy sound from the surface. The black line runs for more than seven miles, and the mountains in the distance are 25 miles away. In more than 100 years, not even the cars that peel off 600-plus mph speed runs have hit them. Over and over, screaming, screeching engines shatter the reverential silence with an alluring rhythmic cacophony, but shortly, graciously, return the playa to blessed tranquility that tempts the mind to wander with awe. (Author's collection.)

Front Cover: Paula Murphy sits atop Walt Arfons's *Avenger* jet-powered dragster. (Courtesy of LandSpeed Productions Research Library [LPRL]/Paula Murphy.)

Upper Back Cover: Stacie B. London works on her race bike. (Courtesy of Kimberly Maroon; see page 70.)

Lower Back Cover (from left to right): Starter Miriam MacMillan releases a speed machine onto the course (courtesy of Zane McNary; see page 87), Nish Motorsports streamliner (courtesy of LPRL/Cris Shearer; see page 22), and Melanie Nish with the Utah Salt Flats Racing Association (USFRA) Club Car roadster (courtesy of Brady Nish; see page 40).

Images of Modern America

BONNEVILLE'S WOMEN OF LAND SPEED RACING

"LandSpeed" Louise Ann Noeth

ARCADIA
PUBLISHING

Published by Arcadia Publishing
Charleston, South Carolina

Printed in the United States of America

Library of Congress Control Number: 2021934588

For all general information, please contact Arcadia Publishing:
Telephone 843-853-2070
Fax 843-853-0044
E-mail sales@arcadiapublishing.com
For customer service and orders:
Toll-Free 1-888-313-2665

Visit us on the Internet at www.arcadiapublishing.com

At five feet, six inches tall, laying in the left nacelle of the fastest car on earth just after it set the first supersonic record at 763 mph, my feet still do not touch the inlet vanes of the ThrustSSC jet engine. My life's nexus is speed. It is intoxicating. Fascinating. It is why I dedicated five years to Save the Salt, a volunteer group desperately trying to reverse decades of federal government mismanagement and restore the Bonneville Salt Flats to safe racing conditions for amateur land speed racers. In my opinion, and from my experience, BLM bureaucrats are the "gorilla glue" of misery that talk like a leaky tire that never gets fixed. (Author's collection.)

CONTENTS

ACKNOWLEDGMENTS

Developing a book like this is a gargantuan treasure hunt. You would not be paging through this taut tome without the gracious, numerous, unrestricted contributions of several key photographers who captured the moments in time shared in this book. I am humbled by their gifts.

Betty Burkland began visually chronicling her family 411 race team in 1969, which included a Studebaker, Datsun, and 400-plus mph streamliner. All of Betty's shots in this book are published for the first time, some 50 years later. She also served as an editor for this book.

Scooter Grubb's skills as a visual craftsman speak for themselves in books, magazines, and hundreds of cherished wall spaces. He is as much a part of the Bonneville Motorcycle Speed Trials as the bikes and riders themselves. The man has the ability to put a soft-touch perspective on badass bikers.

Jim Miller has a visual gift mated to a historical passion for land speed racing—on the dirt, salt, or pavement. More times than are counted, he has had the answer to a question, found a picture I did not know existed, and was a fabulous sounding board on how to unstuck my consternated brain from a dead-end—a consummate historian.

Horst Roesler is a German professional storyteller who rides his way through the two-wheeled world with his collection of cameras, lenses, and evocative compositional ideas both in Europe and the United States. I dare say if it is worth documenting, Horst is there; he often seems to be two places at once. His articles and books are always worth the time you spend.

Cris and Ed Shearer spent 40 years chasing down speed machines in the high-speed shut-off area, ensuring the drivers and riders were A-OK, offering up a glass of cold water before snapping a pic of what was often a major accomplishment moment. She never charged a dime for her work.

Bill Taylor is a veteran racer who is a seriously good, highly organized, sought-after photographer in several motorsports segments. Everything from Bill is always an optical treat.

I am also thankful for the toolbox full of help from Heather Anderson, John Baechtel, Tom Beatty, Robert Beck, Barb Braverman, Burly Burlile, George Callaway, Ron Christensen, Debbie Dannenfelzer, Kat Diamond, Russ Eyres, Pete Farnsworth, Gary Freudenberger, Paul Frocchi, Jalika Gaskin-Sungurtekin, Yoda Gingerelli, Gooding & Company, Tanis Hammond, Sylvia Hathway, Doug Hayes, Jay Hawley, Villa Hizer, Marcia Holley, Ron Hope, Tony Huntimer, Jill Iverson, Joyce (Higbee) Jensen, Laura Klock, Denise Mueller Korenek, Gayle Kott, Professor Leonardo Lanigan, Mick Lanigan, Anne Lindsley, EveAnna Manley, Miriam Macmillan, Pam and Mike Manghelli, Kimberly Maroon, Derek McLeish, Zane McNary, Ky Michealson, Pete Millar Family, Paula Murphy, Brady and Jeff Nish, Olivia and Mike Nish, Gail Phillips, Delvene Reber, Andy Romanoff, Dave Schenker, Bryan Seltzer, Judy and Prozac Sights, Matt Ben Stone, Kristin Stewart, Mike Stewart, Lyn St. James, Anita Strasburg, Dennis Sullivan, Valerie & Danny Thompson, Ed and Linda Van Scoy, Jinx Vesco, Norma Vesco, Vetter Velocity Race Team, Belen Wagner, Dave Wallace Jr., Ellen Wilkinson, and Dan Wright.

INTRODUCTION

The Bonneville Salt Flats are an amphitheater on an utterly colossal scale. They are a dried-out remnant of trapped ocean perched 4,200 feet above sea level along Interstate 80 at the Nevada/Utah border, where seashells are still found in the surrounding mountains hard etched with ancient seashores.

This is America's majestic natural speed laboratory where the starting line symbolizes the incontrovertible nucleus of land speed racing. It is here one must earn the right to present themselves and their speed machine by passing safety and technical inspections before producing glory.

It is here designers, fabricators, and mechanics offer up their handcrafted creations to certified speed traps, hoping to record big numbers on little time slips. It is here, for decades, a fastidious community of volunteers annually labor, lofting a speed village from a desiccated desert, adding a finish line, surveying courses, and roping off a pit area.

Women were forbidden from driving in competition at Bonneville time trials right from the start. The propaganda was dressed up as fear (real or imagined) that if a woman driver was injured in a race car, the entire sport would suffer. And if she were a mother, the terrifying perceived consequences made men shudder.

It took decades, but such parochial wisdom was eventually regarded for what it was: nonsensical. From its start in the late 1920s, the sport had always welcomed women to labor in the speed paradise, but they were forbidden for decades to take part in the joy of tripping the time clocks on the salty speedway, or any speedway for that matter.

Never mind women had been designing and building automobiles and race cars since 1918. Engineer Kate Gleason was the first female member of the Society of Mechanical Engineers, who led her family-owned company to prominence as the nation's top producer of gear-cutting machinery.

In 1953, Robert H. Boyle, author and senior writer at *Sports Illustrated*, commented that "men used cars to deal with sexual insecurities" and that "hot rodding was a sport for lower-middle-class men looking for fulfillment in a world in which the economic system will not allow them to get ahead."

Pretty harsh, but even today, it is one thing to get crushed by a friend, but the idea that a woman might post a faster speed than a man vivisected virility with vestal virgin shockwaves. This may well be a more honest reason why ladies were late to the staging lanes at Bonneville.

None of the above stopped Phyllis Lindsley, mom and grandmother of plenty other racing Lindsleys, from climbing into a "lakester" (then known as a streamliner) at the 1949 Southern California Timing Association (SCTA) inaugural speed trial. She repeatedly drove high-speed passes down the course, assisting chief timer Otto Crocker as he calibrated timing light accuracy. However, she was forbidden from setting any records.

Never has any race car, truck, or motorcycle operated differently due to the operator's gender. All are equally subservient, responsive only to the person handling each. Good input gets good results.

Publicity stunts aside, there is no such thing as a woman or man's speed record: it is a record. Any inference that gender makes some appreciable difference to the outcome is simply ridiculous.

Today, women represent a solid, ever-improving group of land speed racers who ink records in just about any classification they enter. This is particularly evident in the motorcycle classes, where female entries have grown significantly in the past 20 years.

Let us not forget that women have a lower center of gravity that begets better balance and the ability to "crawl under the paint"—especially useful riding high-speed motorcycles.

Women certainly believed themselves risk-takers long before men ever offered up a gracious welcome in motorsports. Women knew that these curmudgeons could no more prevent them from racing than they could stop the earth from spinning on its axis.

Racing suffrage required work. Ginnie Geisler, the wife of an SCTA board member, published an article in the 1971 Speed Week event program noting that her first date with beau Bruce was at an SCTA awards dinner. After they were married, she often went salt racing with him.

"Bonneville was excitingly different," she confessed. "A combination of heaven and hell . . . where I was commanded, reprimanded, sunburnt, windblown, and ignored."

The first seismic participant shift was felt at the 1971 Speed Week when Joy Houston arrived from Gardnerville, Nevada, with a specially prepared motorcycle and was told she would not be able to compete due to her gender—and gender alone.

Already a winning drag racer, Joy and her husband, Art (he was allowed to race), lodged a formal complaint with the American Motorcycle Association (AMA), which sanctioned the motorcycle portion of the SCTA event. The decades-old misogynistic "boys-only" policy was cornered, corralled, and deftly emasculated.

Barbara Braverman's carefully worded article in the 1972 Speed Week event program, on page 32, reports how rookie rider Houston was allowed to race.

Joy was the very first participant down the course, waved off by chief starter Bob Higbee. She rode her 350cc stock-frame Yamaha R5-C and set a Class C-AG record of 109.154 mph using a gas engine modified by none other than multiple world record holder Don Vesco. She bumped up the mark from 100 mph.

How did Houston, seemingly single-handedly, crush more than 100 years of tiny thinking? She simply showed up two years in a row, determined. Knowing the thinking of the day, some might think it more a fairy tale than a reliable historical fact.

Earl Flanders, who was AMA's land speed record steward and District 37 referee at the time, sent the Houstons a letter in March 1972 informing them of a ruling that directed the AMA to allow women to compete at Bonneville, which then forced the SCTA to drop its misogynistic ban.

History pivoted when the following motion was carried at the January 1972 AMA Competition Congress to change Chapter II, Riders and Eligibility, Section A: "All meets must be run with no regard to the sex of the entrant." They also bumped up the record trials sanction to $100 per day.

Dick Rusetta's *Salt Lake City Tribune* article about Houston was picked up by the Associated Press, and suddenly, the whole country knew about the blonde on the bike who was first.

Houston was quoted: "Many men have tried many times to do what I did here today in just one attempt."

It was a decade earlier when Paula Murphy became the first woman to drive a jet-powered dragster at the salt. She had corporate backing led by none other than Andy "Mr. Indy 500" Granatelli.

"Bonneville is a stark landscape with amazing grandeur," said Murphy. "I had the opportunity of participating three times. First, in 1963, as a Studebaker factory driver setting a bunch of production car records that included a woman's two-way record of 161.29 mph driving an Avanti. Next, Barb Neiland and I drove a stock six-cylinder Studebaker Lark for 1,000 miles on a 10-mile circle. We set a USAC record by averaging 103 mph."

She was back on the salt in November 1964 when STP Corporation asked if she might like to go a "bit faster."

"Walt Arfons was already on Bonneville hoping for a new world record with his rocket, but rain stopped that effort," she continued. "Arfons had also brought his 10,000 HP J46 Avenger jet dragster. Although I had never seen, let alone driven one before, I thought, 'why not?' With a borrowed fire suit, I hopped in but could not reach the throttle, the brakes, or the parachute release. A big pillow got stuffed behind my back, and off I went, with only three miles of salt that was not underwater. After 'puddle jumping,' I made the required two-way runs and bumped my personal best record to a 226 mph average with a one-way return run at 243.44 mph. Guess I got a little braver."

Murphy is quick to point out that many individuals and companies led her through an exciting, once-in-a-lifetime career jaunt. She was successful not only in land speed racing, but also was the first woman to earn an NHRA drag racing professional level fuel license. She was the first woman to drive on the famed Indianapolis Motor Speedway. And let us not forget her sports car racing, around-the-world driving, and countless precision driving demonstrations.

"I owe them a great deal and lots of thanks," she said, concluding with, "Hopefully, soon, another woman will surface that will have my career experiences."

Lee (Breedlove) Frank was not as fortunate as Murphy. Despite her flawless driving of the *Spirit of America* jet car, she was blocked from doing her best.

"I would have liked to go faster and have set a higher record, but the sponsors wouldn't allow it," she told me. Momentous will be the day when the world speed crown becomes a tiara.

More than a decade would pass before another woman got a shot at knocking men out of the record books. It was 1978 when Marcia Holley became the first to earn life membership in the male speed bastion known as the Bonneville 200 MPH Club, riding Don Vesco's motorcycle streamliner with a 229 mph two-way average.

"I fell over plenty of times," recalled Holley, who at the time was a dirt bike rider and member of the first all-girl team to race the Baja 500 in the early 1970s, "It took all week to learn how to ride the thing. It was very, very hard because you ride all crossed up. It goes against all your instincts, and at speed, it's all the more frightening."

It had all started on a dare. She was there as a photographer for a bike manufacturer when Vesco offered what became a historic ride. Vesco, and other motorcyclists, had to convince her to race on the salt because it was not her kind of riding, but she was so glad he did.

Afterward, Vesco would often tell her, "You are the best-kept secret in land speed racing." When preparation meets opportunity, intriguing things can occur.

"Most were very supportive, but there was a very small percentage that was against me," she remembered, "It was bad enough to let a woman in the 2-Club, but to do it on a motorcycle streamliner—the hardest land speed vehicle to control—that was even worse.

"Don knew that putting a woman in the 2-Club would twist up some guys with a bad attitude, but he was such a prankster that it was the perfect ploy. As the only woman in the club, it was lonely for such a long time; I am glad to see so many other women now on the membership rolls."

If one only had but a single word to describe Goleta land speed racer Tanis Hammond, it could be nothing else but "effusive." She has a spiritual verve for living that simply splashes all over people.

"I love cars," she said unreservedly. "I really love cars. Love to hear the rumble of a great-sounding engine. Could not wait to turn 16 years old and get a driver's license."

In 1987, she could never imagine the impact on her life from a simple question posed to husband Seth, "Would you ever let me drive the race car?"

"It led to setting my first land speed record on the Bonneville Salt Flats, at 251 mph in 1987," recalled the record-holding racer, a 37-year-old married woman with three small children at the time.

"What am I doing driving a race car?" she thought—and kept going—having the time of her life. In the years that followed, her top speed record reached 323 mph before she stood at the starting line to watch her daughter mash the throttle and ink a 302–plus mph record of her own.

The historical record may forever remain murky on how quickly women joined the sodium speed search because the SCTA only listed the driver by first initial and last name. Absent press reporting, both men and women are poorly served by constipated record keeping. Still, a fine example is Paula Burns, who raced diligently in 2004 to become the first female SCTA national points champion.

It makes one ponder what Vassar College grad Alice Ramsey might make of the pages that follow. This was a lady who, in 1909, wore out 11 sets of fabric tires, making a 3,800-mile transcontinental trip from New York to San Francisco driving a 36HP Maxwell-Briscoe open car, long before a highway system connected the left and right coasts. Did this motorized pioneer cross the salt flats?

What many people do not realize, even today, is that land speed racing is an amateur sport populated with ordinary people who achieve extraordinary things. It does not require loads of experience, money, or connections to take part.

The most welcoming, and easiest way to join is by making runs as a 130 MPH Club participant. Exclusively provided by the Utah Salt Flats Racing Association (USFRA), the class allows spectators to buy an entry number for a few rides down the long black line on the expanse of pure white salt. Sure, there are a few safety details that must be satisfied, but nothing the average person could not put together if they so desired.

Many agree that there is something quite euphoric about getting in line at dawn, and when thundering forth off the starting line, some measure of peripheral vision absorbs the majestic mountains rising and running until the miles squeeze the purples and blues into the horizon line. All who wait are mentally and emotionally charged with anticipation.

When their turn comes to depart, riders and drivers fix their eyes on the distant peak, Floating Mountain, keeping that black line locked in their peripheral vision. Focus is their master, everything else evaporates, and the charge with conviction is on to tickle timing lights where the answer is revealed about how fast they will go.

Spectators usually hear a faint hum and then spy a faint black dot that grows slowly as the explosive sounds of the speed machine make their way down the speedway; first toward the gallery of watchers strung out over five miles, then growing into a recognizable shape, and perhaps showing its colors for a few moments before it rockets off into the distance, growing smaller again until the engine shuts down, parachutes might appear, and silence once more abounds.

Perhaps a record has been set. Perhaps not. But the run is done. The CB radio crackles a quick report out of car speakers about what, who, and how fast. Silence again.

Off to one side is the return road, used by drivers and crews to make their way, slowly, back to the pits. Only the lucky ones, those who have qualified fast enough on the class record, continue on to the impound area and present themselves to make a record run the following morning. Land speed records are not one-shot things. They require a pair of runs where speeds are averaged to determine if the record book gets altered.

The others pull into their pit spot and figure out what must be done to do better the next trip down that black line. Imagination, skill, and yes, hope, all mix up together. When it all unfolds as is hoped, it is as though a symphonic miracle has played out in mechanical form. Men and women alike openly weep for joy, often more a release or permission to exhale and relax in a minor bit of personal glory. The purpose-built speed machine has proven itself to its driver, crew, and all in attendance. Life is so good just then.

Go now, turn page upon page, and meet fabulous females who luxuriate in the sodium spa of speed.

One

FAST FEMALES
ON FOUR WHEELS

Veda Orr gets a helping push start on April 28, 1946, at the first time trial of the year. She recorded a 117.95 mph run to earn 11th in class. Orr was the first woman driver accepted as capable, having started drag racing at Kerney Mesa Air Strip before World War II. Her husband, Karl, is seen pushing on the decklid. (Courtesy of American Hot Rod Foundation/Jim Miller collection.)

Forbidden from competing at Speed Week, the capable and talented Phyllis Lindsley figured out how to drive on the salt at speed. Pictured here, she is climbing in the family Class B streamliner, a narrowed 1927 Ford Roadster with a custom tail section to help chief timer Otto Crocker calibrate the timing lights. (Courtesy of the Lindsley family collection.)

Frankie Beatty tapes up the gaps sealing her husband, Tom, in his hand-built racer made from an aircraft gasoline tank. The couple was a force to be reckoned with in the early days of Bonneville. Beatty clocked 203.6 mph in 1952 using a 1946 flathead block. Note the frayed hat, a gift from a friend that became her favorite sunshade for more than a decade on the salt. (Courtesy of LPRL/ Beatty family collection.)

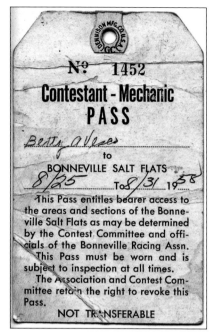

Nº 1452
Contestant - Mechanic
PASS

Betty Vesco

to

BONNEVILLE SALT FLATS

8/25 To 8/31 1958

This Pass entitles bearer access to the areas and sections of the Bonneville Salt Flats as may be determined by the Contest Committee and officials of the Bonneville Racing Assn.

This Pass must be worn and is subject to inspection at all times.

The Association and Contest Committee retain the right to revoke this Pass.

NOT TRANSFERABLE

Betty Vesco led by example, from setting up the family team pit to race prep and starting line tasks. Married to Bonneville pioneer car builder John, they raised two of the fastest boys on the salt. Betty was the final inspector at the starting line who tugged tight on Don and Rick's safety belts. On patrol, if she caught spectators wandering onto the racecourse, she had no problem ordering them back to the spectator area. She not only washed the high-speed parachutes, but also helped pack them back into firing position. She rarely objected when kitchen utensils were liberated for use as shop tools or when the oven was used for baking race car parts. Her birthday was cheerfully celebrated every year on the salt. Daughter-in-law Jinx, also with a race week birthday, has assumed most aforementioned duties. (Courtesy of Vesco family.)

Judy Thompson is pictured being interviewed by Salt Lake City's KSL Radio in 1960. Married to Mickey Thompson, she contributed heavily to every Bonneville record attempt. Whether it was porting engine parts or repairing Mickey's leather driving suit, she got it done. In 2018, the 90-year-old was on the salt to see son Danny set a 448 mph record driving Mickey's refurbished *Challenger II*. (Courtesy of Judy Thompson.)

In 1963, Paula Murphy, 28 years old, with co-driver Barbara Neiland (right), set a 1,000-mile record in a six-cylinder Lark, averaging 100.31 mph. Pictured here is another record-setting model, a Studebaker Commander. The team went on to set a stunning 348 speed and endurance records over a 10-day span driving a dozen different cars; each one was prepared by Andy, Joe, and Vince Granatelli, who also joined in for a bit of the driving fun. (Courtesy of Paula Murphy.)

Nurse Zeldine Graham, married to Athol Graham, helped build the *City of Salt Lake* streamliner powered by the massive surplus World War II Allison airplane engine seen here. After Athol was killed in a brutal crash, she and Otto Anzjon rebuilt and then drove the car on the salt at 254 mph. He died of leukemia the following month, but not before she had given him a reason for a dazzling grin. (Courtesy of Special Collections, J. Willard Marriott Library, the University of Utah.)

In this 1973 photograph, Darlene Russell is hard at work pulling the passenger side spark plugs from the 1953 Studebaker's Chevy V8. Note the plugs already out on the right. Competing in Class E Gas Coupe together with her husband, Dick, and partner Ed Baxter, the trio belongs to the San Diego Roadster Club. (Courtesy of LPRL/Betty Burkland.)

The No. 606 racing roadster was called *Family Affair* for a very good reason: it was driven and maintained by Priscilla (or "Cilla") and Mike Stewart of Bellflower, California. Pictured here in 1981, Cilla, at 31 years old, is climbing in to tow up to the starting line. She clocked 214 mph against Mike's 215 mph record. "It felt good to annoy the men who didn't feel women should drive," recalled her husband. (Courtesy of Mike Stewart.)

Invited to drive the family streamliner, Marcia Holley, who had married Don Vesco, returned to wheel the 444 entry in 1985 to a 272 mph record, bumping up her Bonneville 200 MPH Club mark. A seasoned stunt person in film, Holley had already distinguished herself by earning life membership in the all-guy gang by riding a motorcycle streamliner. (Courtesy of Marcia Holley.)

In 1977, Sandy Haslam began driving *California Girl*, a 1953 Studebaker. She also mixed the fuel, packed the parachute, wired the magneto, and installed drive shafts and quick-change gears. By 1980, she had set a Class D Fuel Coupe record of 188 mph to become the first woman car driver to hold a record on the Salt Flats. Sandy once wrote, "The very worst part of racing is pulling the chute; that means the fun is over!" (Courtesy of LPRL/Betty Burkland.)

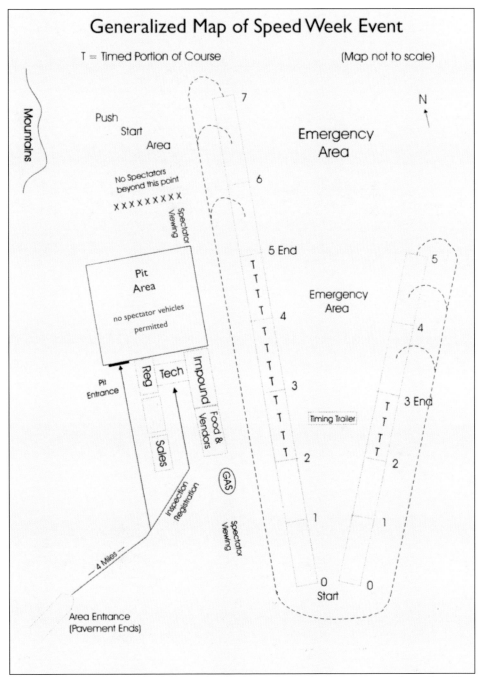

Generalized Map of Speed Week Event

T = Timed Portion of Course   (Map not to scale)

Mountains

Push Start Area

No Spectators beyond this point
X X X X X X X X X

Spectator Viewing

Pit Area

no spectator vehicles permitted

Pit Entrance

Reg   Tech   Impound

Food & Vendors

Sales

Inspection   Registration

GAS

Spectator Viewing

— 4 Miles —

Area Entrance (Pavement Ends)

7

Emergency Area

N

6

5 End

T
T
T
T   4
T
T
T
T
T   3
T
T
T   2

Timing Trailer

1

0
Start

Emergency Area

5

4

T   3 End
T
T
T

2

1

0

Time trials are carefully organized events with strict rules so that racers can feel comfortable and run at full power without running into anyone. Although the layout changes from year to year depending on salt conditions, the starting line is at the bottom of the "V," with a high-speed track on the left and a slower track on the right with the timing tower in the middle. When a racer has a problem during a speed run, if they turn into the center, it alerts the course workers to immediately lock down the racing and send the fire crews and ambulance. Racers and spectators spend most of their time in the pits and along the left side. (Courtesy of LPRL.)

Wendy Jeffries began driving race cars in 1989. Pictured here in 1990, she is posed atop a svelte little lakester powered by a tiny Kawasaki motorcycle engine. By 1993, she took over driving her husband's Corvette and posted a 198 mph top speed that earned her the Fast Lady trophy at the USFRA World of Speed event. Today, she is the editor of *Bonneville Racing News*, a tabloid dedicated to land speed race reports. (Courtesy of Jim Miller.)

Juli Burkdoll, 37 years old, of Ogden, Utah, mother of three sons, stands next to *Pink Thunder*, a family-built streamliner that she drove to a 204 mph record. That was enough to eclipse husband Jim's 203 mph record. She recalled with amusement, "It was exciting and scary as hell at the same time because I found out I was a little claustrophobic." (Courtesy of LPRL/Betty Burkland.)

Pat Zimmerman, 42 years old, and her five daughters are pictured here. Each girl had a job: spotter, timer, communications coordinator, hydration engineer, and cheerleader. Zimmerman, pictured here in 1992, credits her quest to set the Class G Fuel Lakester record at 200.337 mph as a great weight program—she had to maintain 135 pounds to be able to fit in the car with all the safety gear. (Courtesy of Wade Zimmerman.)

For 38 years, Sylvia Hathaway ran the office and the parts department of the Citroen SM World business. It was a global concern. She also wrote stories covering the racing effort for various publications. Building the SM race car was a hobby, but in 1987, it netted Hathaway a life membership in the Bonneville 2 Club when she inked a 202 mph record that stood for 23 years. (Courtesy of Justin Gosaynie.)

Popular cartoonist Pete Millar penned this happy cartoon of Marcia Holley, Tanis Hammond, and Sylvia Hathaway astride a hurtling 200 honoring the trio for their high-speed land speed records. Holley enjoyed horses as much as Hammond loved diving, and Hathaway was the business boss for Citroen SM World. (Courtesy of the Pete Millar family.)

Driving *Salted Peanut* in 1995, Ellen Christensen parked a couple of records in the books driving the turbocharged three-cylinder Chevy Sprint that also netted her the Fast Lady honors at the USFRA World of Speed and again in 1996, driving a Nissan 300ZX. Ellen was also the co-announcer with her husband, Ron, broadcasting on AM 1610 "salt radio," keeping all in attendance informed and entertained. (Courtesy of Ron Christensen.)

No, this is not a Vogue magazine cover shot. Meet Tegan Hammond, atop her parents' gas lakester. The lady drives professionally for commercials, television, social media spots, and films. Tegan's driving career began in 2011 at the Bonneville Salt Flats, where she currently holds two land speed records: 302 mph and 294 mph. (Author's collection.)

When a daughter has a motorhead for a father, it is no surprise that one of the coolest looking, mechanical pieces of jewelry that also doubles as a race car gets built. Thankfully, Seth Hammond is a benevolent dictator who shares the driving with his wife, Tanis, and son Channing as well as other team members. (Author's collection.)

Pam Curtis's odyssey took a few years to become a capable streamliner driver. Pictured here is the Nish Motorsports streamliner. Curtis went from zero to the moment of truth when she racked up a pair of runs that produced a 287 mph land speed record complete with the requisite bottle of champagne. No word as to who was more relieved: the crew or the driver. (Courtesy of LPRL/Cris Shearer.)

Before Pam Curtis could earn her driving privilege at the controls of a 400 mph streamliner, she spent time making licensing runs in open–driver compartment roadsters. The ultra-rookie, assisted by a couple of competent and gracious crews, slowly but surely gained the experience and confidence to strap into the purple powerhouse in 2000. (Courtesy of Mike Nish.)

That is a very satisfied smile on belly tank lakester driver Jerry Kelly, 67 years old, in 2004. She earned her A racing license running in excess of 200 mph and shares the driving fun with husband Jack and son Paul. The body is patterned after P38 fuel drop tanks, so named because the pilot could jettison the tank when empty. (Courtesy of LPRL/Cris Shearer.)

In 2001, Pam Manghelli stepped away from her volunteer duties to license up in hubby Mike's *Cyber Racing* diesel pickup entry. She sat on a pillow because the seat was too hard, so the crew called her "the Diva of Diesel." Her 2002 salt record was 100.542 mph, but she holds the El Mirage 2003 record of 104 mph. (Author's collection.)

Kristin Cline drove her 1955 Studebaker to the salt and then jumped into the race version of the same car, throttling up to 150 mph and earning a pair of 2016 racing licenses. "Nothing else in the world matters when you're on the salt," she professed. "The people, machines, and landscape make it feel like the best of life. One day I'll be there with a car I built myself." (Courtesy of Ethan Cline.)

Susan Christophersen likes to wear Nomex. In 1998, she drove this 1982 Camaro to a 214 mph land speed record. Currently, she and her husband, Steve, drag race a blown alcohol nostalgia funny car called *Susie Q* that often runs a little over 200 mph. Sue drives, and Steve is the engine builder, fabricator, and tuner. (Author's collection.)

The sunrise speedsters pictured here in 2002 are, from left to right, Sue Christophersen, Tanis Hammond, and Dr. Jeannie Pflum; all three women have set speed records in excess of 200 miles per hour. Hammond and Pflum would later carve out 300-plus mph historical records. (Author's collection.)

Miyuki (Wada) Tanakan drove *Dandy Rocket*, a 1986 Mazda RX7, at the 1998 Speed Week, competing in Class E Blown Gas Touring Sports. The team had traveled from Tokyo, Japan, to take part in the 50th golden anniversary. This simple, street-looking car was badly damaged in 2010 when it spun, flipped, and slid upside down at 200 mph—with a man driving. (Courtesy of Bill Taylor.)

Betty Burkland, 62 years old, of Great Falls, Montana, stands next to George Fields's *Trackmaster* competition coupe, in which the grandmother of three drove to a Class E Blown Fuel record of 263 mph, granting her life membership in the Bonneville 200 MPH Club. Assisted by four other teams who stopped racing to ensure Betty got into the record books, some say that is the greater feat. (Author's collection.)

In this 2007 image, master gardener Gail Tesinsky, 53 years old, sits on her 1953 Studebaker, a veteran record-setting car she and her husband, Ron, acquired so that she could have some fast fun. She started off blowing their home-built Hemi engine to smithereens but kept focused and kept making licensing runs until the big day came when she earned the right to drive on the high-speed course. Her best top speed is 221 mph. (Courtesy of LPRL/Cris Shearer.)

Few racers know that Lee Ellen Meiss, driver of the No. 816 gas-modified roadster, is senior vice president/chief transformation officer at Magellan Health, a Fortune 500 company. The salt could not care less about who a person is and what they do—it treats everyone the same. (Courtesy of LPRL/Cris Shearer.)

Linda Van Scoy is the crew chief of a 1985 Corvette driven by husband Ed. From pit prep to fueling and push starting the car off the starting line, she is thoroughly responsible for its safe operation. As the rooster tail of salt flies off the tires, she chases the 240 mph racer five miles down course. And she does all this with a nice manicure. (Courtesy of Ed Van Scoy.)

Former bank executive Tonya Turk races beyond 200 mph yet admits experiencing a lot of anxiety about doing something stupid early in her racing ventures. "If I go out to race, I want to do it right," she said, recognizing setting records demands riveting attention and precision gear shifting. (Courtesy of Cris Shearer.)

At the 2003 Speed Week, driving the *Grumpy Old Men* lakester, rookie Tricia Kisner went from zero to heroine in less than a dozen passes as she spanked all the boys and all the streamliners, setting the top speed of the meet at 317 mph. She remains the first and only woman to earn the *Hot Rod* magazine Top Time Trophy. (Author's collection.)

Dry Lakes Racing Hall of Famer Gail Watson Phillips continually promised her mother that she would stop racing after her next record and promptly broke every one of them. The 202 mph Austin Healey Sprite record came in 1999 and then 205 mph before wheeling a C-5 Corvette beyond 200 mph. Finally, she crashed her new streamliner so gently at 242 mph that she was able to walk away. (Courtesy of Gail and Al Phillips.)

Chick Huntimer, also known as C. Chella Huntimer, adjusts the valves on her V8 Chevy 1928 Ford Roadster in Mentone, California, before checking the head gasket for leaks. Not just a wrench spinner, she deftly handles a paintbrush; note the art on the firewall, which is all her design. Licensed to run up to 200 mph, her top speed is 182. (Courtesy of Tony Huntimer.)

Jerilyn Kugel is pictured at left in a family street roadster turned race car on the Bonneville Salt Flats in 2008. Together with dad Jerry and brothers Joe and Jeff, the quartet drove the car from southern California, some 800 miles, to the salt, swapped out required parts, and sent Jerilyn on her licensing way. On the right is Wendy Hope, delighted to be in the driver's seat. (Left, author's collection; right, courtesy of Rat Trap Racing.)

Chick Huntimer is cruising the 2020 race pits at Bonneville in her roadster, a daily driver that she maintains all by herself. For more than 20 years, she and husband Tony have produced the finest calendar available for the racing community. Despite being a great guy, Tony has only been allowed to drive her rad ride five times in four years. (Courtesy of Tony Huntimer.)

As soon as 300 mph record holder and valet Eric Ritter concludes the requisite shoe cleaning, Rhonnie Vesco, 24 years old, climbs into the family streamliner granddad John built 60 years previously. Two words describe this lady: verve and perspicacity. Rhonnie earned the 2008 Utah Salt Flat Racing Association's Fast Lady trophy for posting a 233 mph speed in command of the historic *Little Giant* streamliner. More fun under the sun came in 2011 with a blazing 310 mph record that not only collected another trophy, but also propelled her into the prestigious 300 mph chapter of the Bonneville 200 MPH Club, joining her father Rick and uncle Don. Mom Jinx and uncle Chuck were the cheering section leadership. (Courtesy of Team Vesco Racing.)

After years of working as a crew member and begging to drive, Andrea (Hoffman) Bello, 30 years old, climbed into Hairball Racing's 1975 yellow Monza, deftly driving 201 mph. With no previous high-speed training, Polish citizen Zofi Peda Proffitt (right) climbed into the land speed racing's fastest type of vehicle, a streamliner, torturing the crew with questions before she clocked a 280 mph record. *Twoje zdrowie!* (Left, courtesy of Andrea Bello; right, author's collection.)

"Running at over 200 mph is a real buzz," New Zealand native Miriam Macmillan recalled without mentioning that her side window blew out past 200 mph, but she never lifted her foot off the throttle. She built her own race car, in which she earned her 200 MPH Club life membership at 204 mph and was the 2010 SCTA National Points Champion while also serving as the Rod Riders Racing Team Club president. (Courtesy of Miriam MacMillan.)

In 2011, at age 71, Mary Hawley had one of the greatest thrills of her life: driving a race version of a Chevy S-10 pickup truck to a record of 132 mph. She qualified for another record at 140 mph, but on the record return run, a rod launched itself out of the engine and it was all over. "Experiencing the thrill of racing is something I will never forget," Hawley claims. (Courtesy of Jay Hawley.)

Heather Anderson has driven this four-speed 1969 Chevy step-side with the 305 engine since 2015 with her dad. Mom Trina Albright is the crew chief and chase truck driver. Best friend Lisa Mossi is part of the pit crew. In 2020, her personal best top speed was 141 mph. Asked why she races, Anderson replied, "All I can say is once you've done it, you won't miss a year." (Courtesy of Heather Anderson.)

Josie Mitcham, a mechanical engineering student at Boise State University, grinds away on a section of the safety cage tubing being installed in the Greenspeed student club 1998 Chevy S-10. This photograph was taken approximately four weeks before the truck passed its safety inspection and competed in 2012 as entry No. 1337 in Class C Diesel Truck. It eventually nailed a 219 mph record in 2017. (Courtesy of Greenspeed/Holly Salewski.)

Victoria Hope, now 26 years old, first drove a race car at 16 when she was a high school sophomore. She holds three land speed records in three different venues and has a top speed of 218 mph. "I do this because it inspires young girls to go out and do the things that they didn't think that they could," she said confidently. "I have proven to myself that I can do absolutely anything I set my mind to and now dream of going 300 mph." (Courtesy of Rat Trap Racing.)

Julia Sheppard Cole races *Fat Ass Herbie* at 2012 World of Speed, managing a top speed of 95.258 mph on the one-mile 130 MPH Club USFRA track. The car was driven roundtrip from Paradise, California, to the Bonneville Salt Flats. *Herbie* was destroyed in the 2018 Camp Fire in California that killed 85 people. (Courtesy of Julia Sheppard Cole.)

When Julia Cole, an educator working with special needs children, took her 2011 vacation with her husband, Juan, the pair drove ocean to ocean in 42 hours, 46 minutes, and 4 seconds. They hold the current Volkswagen Beetle cross-country record, driving 2,920 miles averaging 68.3 mph from New York City to San Francisco. (Courtesy of Burly Burlile.)

Kae Zupan said, "I always try to show, to teach my daughter that women can do anything they set their mind to." To that end, Zupan has her sights set on inking a speed record in excess of 200 mph. "It's good to get out of your comfort zone and try new things. It was one of the best experiences I have had." (Courtesy of Chad Zupan.)

In 2012, Salt Lake City resident Kae Zupan drove this modified roadster, setting a 179 mph record. Kae helps prep the car to race at home, but on the salt, she is very busy with crew duties such as changing the oil, mixing the volatile nitromethane fuel cocktail, and generally doing what needs doing. (Courtesy of Jay Hawley.)

Dixie Rossi is pushing husband Sonny to the starting line on the electric barstool they built together in their San Antonio, Texas, garage. The couple also raced a 1927 Ford Model T modified roadster powered by a Cosworth Vega engine. Dixie is a crack mechanic, fabricator, and consummate crew chief. In 2013, the couple was inducted into the Dry Lakes Racing Hall of Fame. (Author's collection.)

Paula Burns, at 44 years old, was the first woman driver to earn an SCTA national points championship, but it was also a virginal experience for car owners George Callaway and Monte Warnock. In 2004, it was the first time a female wore the crown since the championship began in 1938. "Paula has a natural talent; she can shift the car beautifully through all the gears," observed Callaway, who has been racing since 1954. (Courtesy of Doug Hayes.)

Kaylin Stewart, 18 years old, is pictured in her new fast "2Club" red hat, earned by chasing down a 224 mph land speed record in a blown modified pickup. She went faster than her father, and he could not be happier. "It's just as important to practice slowing down and turning off the racecourse safely as it is to go fast," she explained after conquering fear by replacing it with skill. (Author's collection.)

Great-grandmother Jan Atkinson was 72 years young when she made her Bonneville debut in 2012, setting a 111 mph record in the 36-horsepower challenge at the USFRA World of Speed event. Returning in 2014 with her stick shift "love bug" VW built by husband Wayne, Jan bumped up her record to 119.752 mph. (Courtesy of Burly Burlile.)

Stringfellows have been inking speed records going back 60 years, so it was no surprise when hyper-focused, 16-year-old, third-generation Maddie climbed in the family roadster racer and threw down a 148 mph run past the timing clocks in 2017. It was the very first time she had driven anything by herself. The roaring rookie hopes to blow past 200 mph. (Courtesy of Robert Beck.)

Melanie Nish, 57 years old, of Centerville, Utah, had spent decades supporting her record-setting racing family, but at the 2019 USFRA World of Speed event, it was role-reversal time, and she climbed in a gleaming yellow roadster to earn a series of racing licenses. Pictured here, Melanie inked a top speed of 158 mph. (Courtesy of Brady Nish.)

Jenna Rae Montover, seven years old, the youngest racer in this book, sits in her new junior dragster. "I have been going to the races ever since I was in mommy's tummy," she declared. She wants everyone to know that Papa, Nana, Daddy, Eric, Momma, and her brother Cooper will be her pit crew. On the right is Anita "Nana" Strasburg, who began salt racing in 2019. (Courtesy of Strasburg Family Racing.)

Anita Strasburg, 50 years old, of Mapleton, Utah, has been drag racing since 2006 and now also drives the roaring family lakester. Her first-year top speed was 350 mph. Strasburg narrowly missed setting a record. Note the shredded tire on the rear axle; the lady exercises the throttle to heavy breathing levels. "The ride is unexplainable," she said. "The rush, the nerves, the excitement, and just how badass it is to go that fast." (Courtesy of Strasburg Family Racing.)

Wed to "car nut" Dan in 1972, Kristeen Wright thus began 40 years of salt adventures, first as a USFRA volunteer and then building race cars with Dan before running her Dodge Neon in the 130 MPH Club. Seen here in 2007 with their hand-built streamliner, she snagged USFRA's Fast Lady of the meet with a 219 mph run. It is noteworthy she did it after recovering from a bout with eye cancer. (Courtesy of Dan Wright.)

IndyCar driver Lyn St. James came to the salt in 2007 to drive the *Kansas Twister* gas lakester. Licensing up in three days improved situational awareness and confidence, and despite thundering up to 177 mph on her final run, the car abruptly spun, lightly damaging it. "I've raced SCCA, IMSA, Indycar, off-road, go-karts, FIA, vintage," she confessed. "But nothing compares to running on the salt." (Courtesy of Lyn St. James.)

Racing is part of Megan Volk's DNA, downloaded into her intuitive nature from 60 years of Volk family competition. "It doesn't matter" if you are male or female, she insists. "As soon as you put on the helmet, no one can see who you are; they just notice how well you can drive." (Courtesy of Megan Volk.)

Pictured here are three generations of Volk family racing. Driver Megan Volk, 22 years old, dons her 78-year-old grandfather Larry's five-layer Nomex fire suit as her father (black shirt), Dallas Volk, 51 years old, prepares to start the car. Dallas marvels at Megan's ability to grasp and execute speed deeds faster than most seasoned racers. (Author's collection.)

In 1998, sixty-year-old Judy Sights and husband Bob bought a street roadster. She donned Nomex and became the "knittin' racer," due to her propensity to knock out a sweater while waiting in the staging lanes for her turn to run down the speedway. "I've had nothing but support," noted Sights, now 83, who posted a top speed of 134 mph before she hung up her helmet. (Author's collection.)

Villa Hizer of Rome, Georgia, wanted to feel the rush that her late husband, Courtney, got when he became a 200 MPH Club member in 1987, so her team built a new car and continued the dream for more records. She appreciates Bonneville driving and has reached a top speed of 183 mph in her four-foot-wide 1959 Berkley modified sports car; this southern gal is well on her way. (Courtesy of Villa Hizer.)

The 2019 racing season saw Valerie Thompson assume driving duties of the Treit and Davenport Target 550 streamliner for her first record attempts on four wheels. The 550 team goal is to first break the current conventional wheel-driven, piston-powered automobile-class record of 415.867 mph before heading for 500 mph. (Author's collection.)

Rookie Julie Dollansky managed a two-way average record of 136 mph, but a top speed of 141 mph between the second and third timed mile on the short course. She drove her uncle Jack Slaymaker's 1934 Ford Coupe powered by a supercharged 1950 flathead Ford V8 engine built by her father, Dennis Slaymaker, and Greg White. (Courtesy of Bill Taylor.)

Weber State University student Olivia Nish began racing go-karts when she was eight years old and continued to compete with vigor until age 13, when a national volleyball competition pulled her away. Returning to the family hobby toolboxes, she has become one of the regular working crewmembers. Seen here, she is making her driving debut in a roadster she helped prep. (Author's collection.)

Two

LADY WRANGLERS OF JET-AND ROCKET-POWERED CARS

Perky, petite Paula Murphy, seen here in 1964, became the "World's Fastest Woman on Wheels" after driving 227 mph in Walt Arfons's *Avenger* jet dragster. Murphy went on to motorsports acclaim and was inducted into the Motorsports Hall of Fame, International Drag Racing Hall of Fame, and the Dry Lakes Racing Hall of Fame. (Courtesy of Paula Murphy.)

Paula Murphy is pictured driving on the soaked and swollen salt flats on November 12, 1964. Not using the afterburner, she still averaged 226.37 mph in the mile and 227.38 in the kilo in an open cockpit. Official timing was provided by USAC's Joe Petrali. Both runs were completed in 20 minutes. (Courtesy of Paula Murphy.)

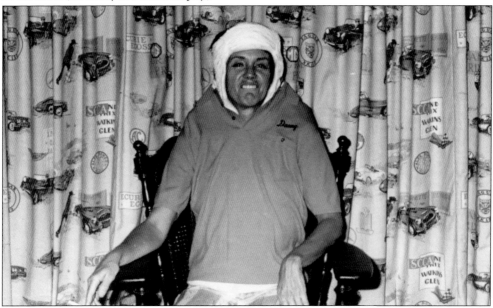

Not every 300 mph high-speed adventure ends with cheers and accolades. When every fuel shut-off device connected to the rocket engine failed to shut down, and the parachutes tore off on the first full-power run in the car built by Ky Michaelson, this was Paul Murphy's aftermath: a full-body cast from her head down to her hips that she wore for four months while recovering from a broken neck in 1973. (Courtesy of Paula Murphy.)

It was 1965 when, on her first time at the controls, Lee Breedlove, 28 years old, drove the *Spirit of America Sonic 1* to a two-way average of 310.14 mph. According to team designer Walt Sheehan, to protect husband Craig's 555 mph record and appease sponsors, the mechanics detuned the jet engine so Lee would be unable to erase her husband's record—not that she did not try. (Courtesy of Lee Frank.)

On September 27, 1965, noted accomplished aviatrix Betty Skelton of Detroit, Michigan, was all smiles before beginning her 277 mph record-setting run in Art Arfons's *Cyclops*. Note the open-face helmet in her hands, the standard head protection that required the use of goggles as an eye shield before full-face helmets were used. Without them, it was impossible to focus at speed because eyelids would flutter. (Courtesy of LPRL/ Firestone News Service.)

It is winter 1965, and Leah Farnsworth stands behind the X-1 rocket car she and husband Pete Farnsworth are building in the family's Milwaukee, Wisconsin, garage. Not just the world's first hydrogen peroxide rocket dragster, it was also the prototype for the *Blue Flame* rocket car that set the 630 mph world record in 1970. Leah was also owner and officer of Reaction Dynamics, the corporation that designed and built both. (Courtesy of Pete Farnsworth.)

A half-century has passed, but the *Blue Flame* rocket car, pictured here on Bonneville Salt Flats, remains the fastest American-built hot rod. USAC timer Joe Petrali so admired co-owner Leah Farnsworth, he allowed her to be in the secure timing trailer as driver Gary Gabelich hurtled into history; she was the first person to know the team had earned the ultimate speed crown on October 23, 1970. (Courtesy of Pete Farnsworth.)

Forced to abandon world record attempts on the Bonneville Salt Flats due to the badly degraded salt crust from years of potash mining that caused the rocket car to break through into the wickedly dangerous briny mud, Kitty O'Neil made her world record mark 512 mph driving the *SMI Motivator* on the Alvord Desert in southeastern Oregon. Her top speed peaked at 618 mph, but it was not part of the record runs. (Courtesy of George Callaway.)

"Deaf people can do anything," Kitty Linn O'Neil once told reporters and proved it repeatedly through the years. The highlight came in 1976, when the five-foot-three, 97-pound half-Cherokee, half-Irish deaf gal out of Corpus Christi, Texas, drove a rocket car that used hydrogen peroxide the way Niagara Falls uses water. Tempered in adversity and for no monetary reward, she easily erased Lee Breedlove's 310 mph mark while restricted to 60 percent of the available throttle. (Courtesy of George Callaway.)

Three

WOMEN RIDERS

Joy Houston, 30 years old, exploded the male myth in 1972 when she became not only the first woman to compete at the Southern California Timing Association's Speed Week, but also set a record at 109 mph. Here, she dons her helmet astride her Yamaha R5-C before another high-speed run. Gardnerville, Nevada, residents Joy and her husband, Art, forced the sanctioning body to dump the misogynistic gender ban with a bit of help from the American Motorcycle Association. "Many men have tried many times to do what I did here today in just one attempt," declared Houston. (Courtesy of Joy Houston.)

World motorcycle record holder Don Vesco thought offering his 21-foot motorcycle streamliner would be a great way to romance stuntwoman Marcia Holley. He was right. To this day, Holley believes her accomplishment of shattering the all-male membership rolls of the Bonneville 200 MPH Club still inspires many women who try on a helmet and fireproof clothing to find out how fast they can go. (Courtesy of Marcia Holley.)

In this 1978 photograph, Marcia Holley strikes a nice PR pose after she cemented a 229 mph record in the historical timeline riding the Kawasaki powered *Lightning Bolt* motorcycle streamliner—the most difficult to control of any land speed racing machine. (Courtesy of Don Vesco.)

Belen Wagner is pictured at left. Teresa (Schmidt) Wagner, at right, became a stepmom to Belen when she married Wiltz, but she was a record-setter in her own right before her mysterious disappearance in 2002. (Left, courtesy of Bill Taylor; right, courtesy of Scooter Grubb.)

Belen Wagner of Mandeville, Louisiana, begged her dad for a motorcycle as childhood pals taught her to ride. At 10, she and her bike had met the wolf—a metaphorical mixture of fear and panic that most know as adrenaline. By 16, in 1987, she began racing on the salt and went on to set 69 national and international speed records in five classes. Her top speed is 219 mph. (Courtesy of Scooter Grubb.)

Crew chief of the Full House Mouse racing team from 1986 to 2010, Gayle Kott also rode a 1955 turbocharged Triumph, wryly dubbed the "Full House Spouse" in 2007, honoring her husband, Fritz Kott. She reprised crew duties for sons Andy, Jason, Chris, and others. President of the San Diego Roadster Club for five years, her book, *Diary of a Racer's Wife*, recounts her multiple racing adventures. (Courtesy of Gayle Kott.)

Southern California resident Cathy Butler learned to ride and began racing in 2001 at age 42. By 2005, she was the first female SCTA national motorcycle points champion. She spent the next 20 years racing multiple motorcycles in multiple classes, including 14 double-duty years as a volunteer event staffer. In 2013, she was voted into the Dry Lakes Hall of Fame. Her personal best on a bike is 201 mph. (Courtesy of Butler Racing.)

Pictured here at the 2011 Bonneville Motorcycle Speed Trials, the premier motorcycle land speed racing event on the salt each year, are 20 women who, over many years and events, have recorded more than 250 land speed records! From left to right are Kathleen Cooke, Jody Perowitz, Julianna (Wallingford) Williams, Belen Wagner, Delissa Bartholome (in white), C. Tucker Allen (behind in hat), E. Hakansson, Erin Sills, Christine (Freeman) Howard, Michelle Mielke, Tiadra Simmermon, Erica Cobb, Karlee Cobb, Laura Klock, Leslie Porterfield, Valerie Thompson, Karena Markham, Tracey Snyder, Kim Krebs, and Lucille Dunn. (Author's collection.)

Cayla (Rivas) Kaolelopono, 18 years old, at left, is a prolific American motorcycle racer based in Fresno, California, who set the FIM world record by reaching a speed of 252 kph, riding a modified Royal Enfield 650cc Twin at the 2018 Bonneville Motorcycle Speed Trials (BMST). On the right, in 2014, Loretta Flores, 22 years old, a graduate of the Motorcycle Mechanic Institute, has a personal best top speed of 204 mph. (Courtesy of Scooter Grubb.)

In Jody Perewitz's supportive motorcycle riding family, it was predictable that she embraced two-wheelers. Through the years, her skills were honed, and accolades were accumulated. In 2011, the rookie salt rider rode to a 203 mph world record. Dad Dave was an elf on her shoulder for every inch of the course, whether she admits it or not. (Author's collection.)

Meet Leslie Porterfield, who began riding and racing motorcycles at 16. By 2008, the American Motorcyclist Association named her Racing Female Rider of the Year. The year before, at 227 mph, a tumbling crash broke seven ribs, punctured a lung, and gave her a concussion, but did not break her competitive spirit. (Courtesy of Horst Roesler.)

It is interesting that rider Leslie Porterfield's bike number is also the year of her birth. Seen here in 2009, Leslie is blasting past the pit area, attempting to set another speed record. She earned three land-speed records and is a member of the Bonneville 200 MPH Club. Her top speed is 232 mph. (Courtesy of Scooter Grubb.)

Since 2007, Jalika Gaskin-Sungurtekin has been the crew chief of the Alp Racing Design Team that has set a number of land speed records with vintage Triumph engines reworked to stunning speed and performance levels—all visually inviting. Together with her rider and husband, Alp, she discovered something wonderfully encouraging and self-propelling about being responsible for the intimate understanding and operation of a salt racer. Recently retired *Asymmetric Aero* hit 175 mph and is now on display in the Haas Moto Museum in Dallas, Texas. The skills and knowledge base she has acquired now allow her to build a remote village to tackle far horizons. To that end, the couple is working on a new bike with a very old powerhouse: a 1948 Vincent HRD. Courtesy of Kimberly Maroon.)

Multiple record-setter Karina Markham is on the left and races with these high-speed braids. On the right is mechanical engineer Kristin Stewart, with three records aboard her Honda, the *Sherminator*. She founded the Bonneville Land Speed Racing Women Facebook page. (Left, author's collection; right, courtesy of Dan Kaplan.)

On the left is Cindi Turgeau, a rider and volunteer. On the right is a multiple record setter C. Tucker Allen. (Both, courtesy of Horst Roesler.)

More than 20 records were set by Klock Werks women in leathers from 2006 to 2012. From left to right are Michelle Mielke, mom Laura Klock, and daughters Erika Cobb and Karlee Cobb, who, at age 14 in 2008, was the youngest salt record-setter. Together, the history-etching trio was the first mother and daughter team to set records at the same time during the same event on the salt. (Courtesy of Scooter Grubb.)

Laura Klock of Mitchell, South Dakota, has ridden many bikes on the salt flats, including this Victory Vision on which she set a 123 mph record to prove that "big road bikes can also be fast, not just comfortable, and women can ride them too." Klock is also responsible for developing the patented Klock Werks FLARE windshield that adds stable downforce to racing salt bikes. (Courtesy of Klock Werks/Dave Sietsema.)

Pictured here, Tracy Snyder's eyes filled with tears as she realized that after four grueling, worry-filled days, she had set a new national land speed record in Bonneville at 171 mph. Her unofficial slogan is "Life begins at 40, but it gets interesting at 150 mph." (Courtesy of Scooter Grubb.)

As Tracy Snyder, seen here, prepared for the ride of a lifetime on her tricked-out Hayabusa record-setting motorcycle, a wake of admirers followed every twist of the throttle and squeeze of the brakes. "This isn't just about me," she told her twin sister, Andra. "In racing, you can't be successful by yourself. It's a team effort." (Courtesy of Horst Roesler.)

Rebecca Berneck has come a long way since buying her dainty Italian Vespa scooter. While she is CEO of a company she founded and a former dancer in a film featuring the singer Prince, standing here on the salt with her vintage BMW motorcycle, the only business she is doubtless mulling over is which land speed record to set next. (Courtesy of Scooter Grubb.)

This three-wheeled speed machine *Killajoule* was a rather expensive hobby powered by nanophosphate batteries and driven by Swede Eva Hakansson to a 270 mph land speed record. According to the rookie rider, she was responsible for 80 percent of the vehicle fabrication. (Courtesy of Horst Roesler.)

Erin Sills is the progenitor of the SheMoto scholarship given at each BMST awards ceremony that recognizes a participating woman who embodies camaraderie, sportsmanship, fortitude, perseverance, patience, leadership, and the desire to win. The recipient receives $1,000 for herself and another $1,000 to give to an individual or organization that has served as a source of encouragement in her racing. (Courtesy of Scooter Grubb.)

Erin Sills's first record came courtesy of Jack Costella's *Nebulous Theorem 5050*. Lying on her stomach, Sills piloted the 14-inch-tall, 14-foot-long rocket to 143 mph with a tiny 80cc motor. Named the 2014 AMA Female Athlete of the Year, Erin is a 25-time land speed world and national record holder, and three-time Guinness World Record holder, often running in excess of 200 mph. (Author's collection.)

Denise Mueller Korenek owns the eye-popping 183 mph paced bicycle land speed record set on September 16, 2018. Before you think this is some crazy stunt, know that a bicyclist rode behind a train in 1899 using its draft to be timed at 60 mph. Further, this gal with the genial grin has eclipsed the records of 10 men riding under her Project Speed banner. (Courtesy of Matt Ben Stone.)

Pace car driver Shea Holbrook and Denise Mueller Korenek have a symbiotic relationship communicating throughout the run via lights and video feeds. Shod in a leather and Lycra racing suit aboard the hand-built custom ride, Denise was pedaling for 3.75 miles under her own power. Holbrook is driving a 1,000-horsepower lakester with the aluminum fairing Denise relies on for speed and stability. (Courtesy of Matt Ben Stone.)

Two core Project Speed teammates, pace car driver Shea Holbrook (left) and bicycle racer Denise Mueller Korenek are all smiles after setting the new world record together on the famed salt flats despite its deteriorating surface condition. (Courtesy of Matt Ben Stone.)

Stunning describes the Gear Grinders Racing Club member Connie Sulu Beavers-Nicolaides. As comfortable in excess of 200 mph as she was strolling down the street, Beavers-Nicolaides is remembered by the racing fraternity as never having an unkind word to say about anyone. The girl lived serious golden years until 2015. (Author's collection.)

At 74, Connie Sulu Beavers-Nicolaides dropped jaws as she rolled off the starting line astride her Suzuki Hayabusa (Japanese for "peregrine falcon") and bespoke color coordinated helmet and leathers. She campaigned the two-wheel mean machine with her 82-year-old husband Nick Nicolaides astride his matching ride. (Author's collection.)

Convivial Connie Beavers gets last minute instructions from the starter. It is noteworthy that her stylish safety gear is color coordinated with her jet-black mascara. (Author's collection.)

Stacie B. London is connected, possessed of "in the moment" perception, and a sense of purpose that radiates out to all around her. With years of mentorship from the late Ralph Hudson of Ironwood Racing renown, she repays the gift with her volunteer service as a motorcycle safety inspector doing Hudson proud. (Courtesy of Kimberly Maroon.)

Stacie B. London explains to spectators the joy she derives from racing motorcycles. Note the Ford pickup, London's salt workhorse on the flats. (Courtesy of Kimberly Maroon.)

Stacie London has five land speed records—two that she set on the flats, a place where she not only needs to be, but where she seeks encounters with others as passionate as she is about mechanical art. Here, aboard her *Triple Nickel* entry, she again starts to coax more miles per hour out of a single-cylinder vintage motorcycle than most would ever think possible. (Courtesy of Andy Romanoff.)

This is not Erin Sills, but Oklahoman Sherry "Fuzzy" Soliz, who comes to the sport as a 2016 AMA national record holder and now rides a 1956 BMW R60 in Class PPC-650 that first belonged to her father. She, and the bike she races, are the same age. Off the bike, Fuzzy volunteers as a starter, sponsor, and volunteer recruiter. (Courtesy of Scooter Grubb.)

Jennifer Medlin knows she was blessed to achieve her personal speed goal of 150 mph on her 2014 Harley Davidson Low Rider—150.642 mph, to be exact. This came after she rolled up more than 50,000 miles on it as a daily rider, including 2,600 miles roundtrip from Marion, Louisiana, to Bonneville. (Courtesy of Jennifer Medlin.)

Meet monkey Nida Murray. Not in any way a slur, it is her official team position aboard the *Suicycle* sidecar motorcycle, where she uses her entire body as a counterweight and traction agent a mere few inches off the ground. (Courtesy of Scooter Grubb.)

Few married couples have the hobby that Nida and Rick Murray spend time on. As Team RGM, Rick holds the handlebars and controls the throttle and brakes while wife Nida, the monkey rider, merely hangs on for dear life, head down and a few inches from a pair of whirling back wheels. Love takes many forms, and they have won several North American sidecar road racing championships. (Courtesy of Scooter Grubb.)

Kim Krebs's spirit is indomitable; she understands that motorcycle racing is equal parts rider and bike. "I'm an equal, along with everyone else who braves this pursuit," says the record-setting lady who believes going fast is more meditative than terrifying. "We're all people, and we all have something to offer each other." (Courtesy of Scooter Grubb.)

Here arrives the magic moment for Kim Krebs and her Black Art Racing speed machine; the clocks have her in their grip and will announce without malice or emotion how fast they have gone this time down the track. The 1999 Suzuki GSXR 750 has carried her to a 241 mph record and a personal-best top speed of 244 mph. (Courtesy of Scooter Grubb.)

In 2013, encouraged by fellow riders and bewitched by the salt, Sandy Vetter, from Crows Landing, California, started racing when she was 75. She set five land speed records (AMA No. 1 plates) with the same bike and retired at age 80 in 2018. Husband Chris kept her 1972 Yamaha R5 350cc in race-ready condition under the Vetter Velocity banner. (Courtesy of Sandy Vetter.)

Volunteer starter Kari Amundsen of Missoula, Montana, green flags the riding marvel Elana Meyers, a factory Triumph rider astride a production rocket. Meyers was the first woman to win a professional motorsport event at Daytona International Speedway in 2010. (Courtesy of Horst Roesler.)

Most any other time, Valerie Thompson is a hotshot motorcyclist, but the star of this shot is Reckon, and she is a dutiful "dog mom." For reasons only Reckon knows, he always loved being inside her helmet from his earliest puppy days. (Courtesy of Horst Roesler.)

Scottsdale, Arizona, resident Valerie Thompson is behind her 389-pound BMW S 1000 RR, with which she earned five records and a top-speed personal best of 217 mph. (Courtesy of Horst Roesler.)

Valerie Thompson, 53 years old, is an eight-time land speed record holder who can honestly claim "World's Fastest Female Motorcycle Racer" bragging rights when, in 2018, she inked a 328 mph record piloting a motorcycle streamliner, setting the latest in a long string of records riding traditional two-wheelers. (Courtesy of Scooter Grubb.)

Kat Diamond from Los Angeles, California, calms her nerves by tuning into the engine's voice and finds its vibration settling. She admits hearing a voice from the god of speed welcoming her to the salt. "I love the space where I and motorcycles can run in the wilderness on this incredible earth," she professes. She has an abiding love of the beautiful horizon and the large-scale sky. (Courtesy of Kat Diamond.)

Kat Diamond beams in the setting sun, posing with her Honda CB160 race bike. "As long as my life lasts and I can ride a motorcycle, I will return to the salt," she declares. "It is exactly my pleasure." Her personal-best record is 81.353 mph. (Courtesy of Kat Diamond.)

Kathleen Cooke, from Cleveland, Ohio, riding her 50cc Honda, has just entered the timed portion of the track, on her way to another record. Her favorite record was in 2013, when she posted a mile-per-hour that was larger than the cubic centimeters of her production engine. Together with husband Louis, they are in charge of rider orientation. (Courtesy of Scooter Grubb.)

Involved in the sport for 16 years, Jill Iverson of Prescott, Arizona, has ridden motorcycles most of her life. She currently races a 1941 suicide shift Indian (a 50th birthday present built by husband Dave), upon which she has set five records. The top-speed record is 106 mph. "Land speed racing is the perfect competition for me because it's me against the clocks," says Jill, effusive with joy. (Courtesy of Doug Hayes.)

In a lovely turnabout of race duties, "umbrella boy" Dr. Glenn Freudenberger dutifully shades rider Nancy Wennerberg on the starting line in 2009. She and her husband, Jon, have ridden a variety of bikes on the salt, setting records in different classes through the years. Nancy has inked a record at 202 mph. (Author's collection.)

Four

UNSUNG HEROINES

For more than a decade, most people met the effervescent Linnea Johnston, "the Trailer Queen," this way: through the registration window at the BMST operations trailer. A longtime motorcycle rider and racing enthusiast, she is an integral part of the planning and operation of every speed meet. After promising her husband to stay in double digits, she inked a 113 mph time slip astride a Buell. (Courtesy of Scooter Grubb.)

For decades, Vera and Multy Aldrich were Speed Week's official "Mr. & Mrs. Hospitality" who greeted visitors at the end of the paved road that dropped them onto the flats. Vera's gift of fresh-baked cookies and coffee endeared her to all arrivals. She was not an event promoter but a sincere friend of its participants and spectators. (Courtesy of LPRL/Miriam and Jim Deist.)

Vicky "Hawkeye" Spring beams with joy. She holds the beloved Vera Aldrich award, at one time given to those who serve unselfishly. In the race car shop, she could always find misplaced anything and learned how to weld and use the plasma cutter to make racecar parts. Vicky also drove a couple of land speed cars, more to peg her "fun meter" than set records. (Courtesy of Monte Warnock.)

Meet Mary West, who was considered the backbone of the Utah Salt Flats Racing Association. She was possessed of a big heart and ready smile. As the first secretary for USFRA, she kept track of everything—her home was the club's office. She also labored for 20 years as a secretary with the land speed racing advocacy group Save the Salt. "The future of the Bonneville Salt Flats remains in the hands and hearts of those of us who care," she noted. West also owned and drove boats and drag raced cars. At Bonneville, she reached a top speed of 222 mph, for which she earned the USFRA's World of Speed Fast Lady award. She also wrote for many national racing publications. (Courtesy of Betty Burkland.)

Guardian volunteer Anne Lindsley is on duty in the timing tower, recording every speed generated from every timing segment of every speed machine—by hand. She is the human backup. A stickler for the rules, many agree she can be counted on for organizing and streamlining a process or procedure. A 50-year member of the Gear Grinders Car Club, she is also competent on horseback. (Author's collection.)

Ellen Wilkinson's role in the Utah Salt Flats Racing Association is like a diamond: multifaceted. Her duties include clerical and financial aspects of the membership rolls, race vehicle registration, legal document preparation for government agencies, speed record certificates and trophy preparation, all merchandise aspects, and coordinating meetings and special activities. (Courtesy of Ellen Wilkinson.)

Debbie Dannenfelzer, 55 years old, of Santa Barbara, California, daughter of land speed racers Patty and "Fast" Fred, has volunteered every year this century at Speed Week in various roles. Now the Bonneville chief timer, it is her voice over the CB radio announcing which racer is on course, the speeds, and ancillary details about the run. (Courtesy of Shari Polk.)

Joyce Jensen, married to chief starter Jim Jensen, is the daughter of Bob Higbee, a lynchpin founder of Speed Week since 1949. Her good penmanship skills at age 10 started her volunteer work writing racer's timeslips. With a few years off to raise two sons, the woman is still helping out in the registration trailer. (Courtesy of Cris Shearer.)

Cris Shearer, together with her husband, Ed, spent 40 years chasing racers in the high-speed shutdown segment of the racecourse. Their selfless service included a cool drink to the driver and snapping a quick "elation moment" photograph that she later mailed to each participant. (Courtesy of Bill Taylor.)

By deed, not braggadocio, Miriam MacMillan became a respected SCTA vice president, Save the Salt advisory board member, Rod Riders Racing Team Club president, and the 2012 Bonneville Nationals chair. (Courtesy of Zane McNary.)

Speed Week assistant starter Jill Iverson works in lockstep with chief starter Jim Jenson. Here, she holds a racer at the starting line as she talks with timing tower staff about course conditions. Before any racer departs the starting line, Jill must be satisfied all is 100 percent with racer and machine. She is also the SCTA treasurer, an elected position. (Courtesy of Paul Frocchi.)

USFRA chief timer and "Juli of all Trades" Burkdoll has total control of the entire racecourse, race stewards, starting line personnel, and rescue crews and is in constant communication with all. She continually updates data for every racer in every class. For decades, the Burkdoll family has been part of every aspect of event prep, operation, and cleanup. (Courtesy of Juli Burdoll.)

Speed Week volunteer Lois Oppermann would arrive at the timing tower at dawn and not leave until the last piece of paper was filed away, usually after sunset. Lois and her husband, Bob, were on-site and active for decades. (Courtesy of Tony Oppermann.)

In this 2008 photograph, event manager Delvene Manning (now Reber) is conducting motorcycle racing business during the annual speed meet as eight-month-old son Jack admires the scenery. The thick notebook is evidence of the bazillion details that are part of keeping things running smooth and safe. Note the FM walkie-talkie in her side pocket that monitors all on-track activity. (Courtesy of Horst Roesler.)

Judy and Glenn Zeretzka, from Arroyo Grande, California, have volunteered to work at every BUB International Motorcycle Speed Trial–turned–Bonneville Motorcycle Speed Trial ever held, beginning in 2004. All this despite a severe sun sensitivity, and yet the organizers now rely on both to help train newcomers. (Courtesy of Scooter Grubb.)

Judy Sights, also known as "the Bag Lady," scrutinized all safety gear and entry documentation in the inspection lines before any speed machine was reviewed technically. For years, she also kept SCTA finances straight as the two-term SCTA treasurer and is now shepherdess of the scholarship program. (Author's collection.)

Team pit boss Jinx Vesco first went to the salt in 1967, newly married to Rick Vesco, and began a 50-year volunteer journey that included the founding of the Utah Salt Flats Racing Association and Save the Salt advocacy group, working with federal and state elected officials for years as well as late-night, 250-mile recon trips checking the salt conditions. (Courtesy of Jinx Vesco.)

Before Air Commodore Jayne Millington of the British Royal Air Force was presented to Queen Elizabeth II for distinguished service, she was the "Voice of Black Rock" in 1997, when the first supersonic land record was inked. Daily, she communicated on six different radios and telephones, tracking who was where and why on the wall map. Jayne ensured the desert was clear when the howling jet car ran. (Author's collection.)

At this point, one might be "blown away" by the many ladies in this book. The list that follows represents the substantial contributions made by women in helmets, record books, toolboxes, and service providers. Rest assured, the preceding smiles are the result of far more than good dental hygiene. (Courtesy of Betty Burkland.)

LAND SPEED LADIES

Each of these women has earned the right to present themselves and their speed machine on a Bonneville Salt Flats starting line. Before they departed said starting line, they donned the requisite safety clothing and helmet and then climbed in or on their chosen ride. Some accelerated with conviction simply to peg their "fun meter" or check off a bucket list line item. Others seriously assaulted a standing record and were intent on rolling up big numbers whistling through the timing lights. All were spectacular. To be clear: the joy was the same regardless of what mark was etched, and the speed was secondary to the accomplishment.

Arlene Acton
Trina Albright
C. Tucker Allen
Heather Anderson
Teresa Anderson
Felicia Anderson-Sean
Jan Atkinson
Veronica Bailye
Virginia Balcourt
Susan Balthaser
Carla Barajas
Delissa Bartholomew
Theresa Bates
Connie Beavers
Andrea (Hoffman) Bello
Rebecca Berneck
Petra Bier
Jaylin Billing
Heather Black
Michelle Brading
Lee Breedlove-Frank
Charisse Buchta
Juli Burkdoll
Betty Burkland
Paula Burns
Cathy Butler
Leslie Cadwallader
Roxann Caisse
Inez Carlson

Madeline Carlson
Tracie Carroll
Brenda Sue Carver
Barbara Chilson
Ellen Christensen
Pat Christensen
Susan Christophersen
Linda Clark
Kristine Cline
Erica Cobb
Karlee Cobb
Julia Cole
Lillian Conboy
Penny Cook
Kathleen Cooke
Danielle Cote
Elans (Myers) Court
Lisa Curtis
Pam Curtis
Sarah Curtis
Joy Dahlberg
Gloria Dalton
Karen Davis
Allison (Volk) Dean
Celia Dean
Nadine DeFreitas
Kat Diamond
Julie Dolansky
Robin Dripps

Debbie Dross
Cecille Dunn
Lucille Dunn
Diana Dunning
Nadine Endacott
Valerie Fenn
Norma Fergus
Amanda Ferguson
Loretta Flores
Hayley Freudiger
April Froke
Annie Fyie
Maria Gerber
Suzanna Green
Caitlin Gray
Wende Greenleaf
Donna Grippen
Debbie Gussenhoven
Eva Hakansson
Tanis Hammond
Tegan Hammond
Irene Hanchard
Tonya Harding
Sandy Haslam
Sylvia Hathaway
Mary Hawley
Katrina Herbert
Kathy Hickey
Villa Hizer

Marcia Holley
Leslie Hoogerhyde
Dianne Hope
Victoria Hope
Joy Houston
Leesa Houston
Cheri Howard
Christine (Freeman) Howard
Marci Howey
C. Chick Huntimer
Kate Ingber
Jill Iversen
Wendy Jeffries
Joyce (Higbee) (Dalton) Jensen
Monique Johansson
Carla Johnson
Cissy Johnson
Linnea Johnston
Racheal Johnson
Norma Kastien
Renee Kaehny
Geri Kelly
Dianna Kenny
Cayla (Rivas) Keolelopono
Rachel Keown
Leona Kephart
Kae Kinomoto
Laura Klock
Denise (Mueller) Korenek
Gayle Kott
Kim Krebs
Jerilyn Kugel
Wendy (Hope) Landsiedel
Sarah LePetri
Pattie Lindsley
Phyllis Lindsley
Melissa Logue
Stacie B. London
Ruth Lundring
Ruth MacLean
Suzanne MacDonald
Miriam MacMillan
Pam Manghelli
Charlotte Manning
Karena Markham
Kelly Marshall
Lynn Marshall
Holly Martin
Syndee Martin
Jennifer Medlen
Lee Ellen Meiss
Andrea Metos

Michelle Mielke
Vicki L. Miley
Jozey Mitcham
Samantha Morgan
Paula Murphy
Leslie Murray
Nida Murray
Dr. Roberta Nichols
Barbara Nieland
Melanie Nish
Olivia Nish
Louise Ann Noeth-Lanigan
Kitty O'Neil
Erin Okonek
Cynthia Oliphant
Fina Olsen
Gina Morill Olsen
Lyn Neale Olsen
Veda Orr
Keriann Ortiz
Tabitha Ott
Kaylin Patterson
Kristine Peach
Zofi Peda-Proffitt
Jody Perewitz
Shelly Petersen
Diane Pettijohn
Dr. Jeanie Pflum
Gail Watson-Phillips
Lucia Phinney
Heidi Pitkin
Leslie Porterfield
Marge Price
Shana Rameriez
Natasha Ranger
Susan Robertson
Lee Sable
Jessica Sadler
Annie Sam
Rhonda Samarin
Evelyne R. Scholz
Tricia (Kisner) Shaffer
Judy Sights
Erin (Hunter) Sills
Tiadra Simmermon
Trisha Simpson
Betty Skelton
Anna Skurdal
Marjorie Smith
Tamara Smith
Linda Snyder
Tracy Snyder

Sherry Soliz
Vicky Spring
Lyn St James
Deanna Stagner
Carol Stahman
Shelia Stang
Beth Stenmark
Janel (Thompson) Sternoff
Annette Stewart
Kaylin Stewart
Kristen Stewart
Priscilla Stewart
Cheryl Strasberg
Anita Strasburg
Madelyn Stringfellow
Jeanne Talbot
Miyuki (Wada) Tanakan
Karen Teerlink
Gail Tesinsky
Valerie M. Thompson
Donna Timney
Mary True
C. Allen Tucker
Elise Tucker
Cindi Turgeau
Tonya Turk
Angela Vaughn
Rhonnie Vesco
Sandy Vetter
Sharon Vickery
Megan Volk
Belen Wagner
Donna Wagner
Teresa Wagner
Nancy Wennerberg
Mary West
Shari West
Brooke Widdison
Julianna (Wallingford) Williams
Susan Wilson
Ashley Woodford
Linda Wortman
Kristeen Wright
Katie Young-Cortez
Ali Youngblood
Ginger Zehm
Pat Zimmerman
Kae Zupan

Without the ladies listed below, the drivers and record setters perhaps would have no starting line from which to begin the speed adventure. It is important to note that although a man might have held the elected position at the sanctioning body, it was a woman who did the work, most often a wife.

"Mom kept books for SCTA for many years," confessed son Phillip Grisotti amusedly about his mother, Madeliene. "Dad just took all the credit."

Volunteers are the heart and soul of amateur land speed racing. Nearly all labor out of love for a family member or simply to help friends. Together, they form a congenial safety and adventure net for the entire sport.

Linda Ainge	Dottie Higbee	Lois Opperman
Vera Aldrich	Lila Hodson	Ann Peacock
Kari Ammundson	Emily Howey	Delvene Manning-Reber
Frankie Beatty	Erin Howey	Delia Riley
Barbara Braverman	Liz Howey	Dixie Rossi
Jan Callaway	Marci Howey	Carolyn Sager
Mary Carson	Mary Hoyt	Cris Shearer
Kathye Collier	Harly Legowski	Beverly Smith
Kristy Cook	Dawn Kennedy	Bev Stanley
Victoria Corredoira	Cherie Knotts	Judy Thompson
Keiko Costella	Jenisa Knotts	Valerie (Taylor) Thompson
Debbie Dannenfelzer	Julie Levie	Linda Van Scoy
Judy Dean	Michele Levie	Betty Vesco
Leah Farnsworth	Shari Lattin	Jinx Vesco
Pauline Ferguson	Anne Lindsley	Norma Vesco
Marge Francisco	Pamela Lubell	Amanda Volk
Jalika Gaskin-Sungurtekin	Doris (Stinson) Lutes	Angie Volk
Claire Gee	EveAnna Dauray Manley	Judy Volk
Ginnie Geisler	Dorothy McClure	Joanie Warner
Emily Gillette	Tammy (Barrett) McDowell	Ellen Wilkinson
Zeldine Graham	Jayne Millington	Judy Zaretska
Madeleine Grisotti	Cheri Notts	

BIBLIOGRAPHY

Batchelor, Dean. *The American Hot Rod*. St. Paul, MN: MBI Publishing Company, 1995.

Bouzanquet, Jean-Francois. *Fast Ladies: Female Racing Drivers 1888–1970*. Dorchester, UK: Veloce Publishing Ltd., 2009.

Kasprowicz, Sarah. *The Reluctant Rocketman: A Curious Journey in World Record Breaking*. Waukesha, WI: Green Bean Creative Solutions LLC, 2013.

Noeth, Louise Ann. *Bonneville Salt Flats*. St. Paul, MN: MBI Publishing Company, 1999.

———. Images of America: *Bonneville Salt Flats*. Charleston, SC: Arcadia Publishing, 2020.

Rosler, Horst. *Bonneville: World's Fastest Motorcycles*. Stillwater, MN: Wolfgang Publications Inc., 2007.

DISCOVER THOUSANDS OF LOCAL HISTORY BOOKS
FEATURING MILLIONS OF VINTAGE IMAGES

Arcadia Publishing, the leading local history publisher in the United States, is committed to making history accessible and meaningful through publishing books that celebrate and preserve the heritage of America's people and places.

Find more books like this at
www.arcadiapublishing.com

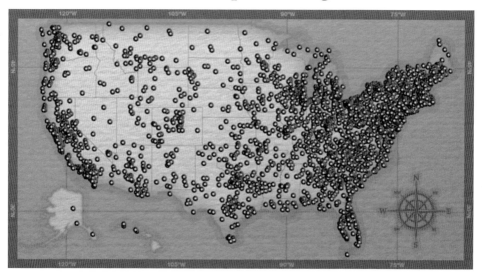

Search for your hometown history, your old stomping grounds, and even your favorite sports team.